Becoming Pagan

By Ty Jamie Coxston

Green Magic

Green Magic
5 Stathe Cottages
Stathe
Somerset
TA7 0JL
England

www.greenmagicpublishing.com
info@greenmagicpublishing.com

Typeset by Green Man Books, Dorchester
greenmangallery@lineone.net

ISBN 978-0-9561886-4-9

GREEN MAGIC

I

Preface

This is not Path specific, only an aid to begin, re-start or continue along your way. Even to help you discover what is not right for you.

Even if you do not wish to label your path, there are no hard and fast rules or scripture (this can be a problem for some beginners), you just need to follow your heart. Here at least is the Calendar, some helpful guidance and advice, ways and means to meditation and the all important networking, whether you wish to follow a solitary path, find a coven or set up your own network.

Ty has a science Honours degree in social sciences and a post graduate degree in Education, qualifying her to teach, but more importantly she is already an author on the environment and spiritual living, a Pagan Priestess (appointed title), a Pagan Chaplain and a teacher of Paganism, the craft and herbs. She works with new Pagans on a daily basis. Ty is also a Pagan minister helping Pagans abroad by correspondence. She grows a great deal of her own herbs, food and medicine, there is no definitive line between her life style and her faith as they are one.

Dedication

First of all I need to thank and acknowledge Mr Kevan Manwaring, for a writing workshop I attended many; many years ago as from there I became the bard I am today. His talk and teaching encouraged my poetry to flow, like releasing a flock of birds from a cage. On that same weekend I met Mrs Susan M Phillips to whom my thanks will never find sufficient words. She is a part of my soul, and co-author of our first book 'Green Living Sacred Life', it was her who shook the author tree within me and let the apples of inspiration fall.

I also wish to thank Tony for his boundless support and wisdom, my Parents for more than I could ever write – they have 'rescued' me so many times and still turn up in many an hour of need.

I wish to thank Mr Andy Harrop Smith for guiding me to my Druid Path and Wendy Shrubshaw for her inspiration in keeping me there as well as the bounty of her energy. She has inspired me to run my own workshops.

I want to thank everyone that has been, and is, a part of my life for each individual has aided me to take the steps to bring me here to this glorious dance of life, and this book.

Finally a special thankyou to the prison service for employing me and all my Anglican Ministers that are my bosses! Thank you to all the Pagan Prisoners past, present and future for your unbounded thirst for knowledge and for pushing me to research and create the foundations for this book.

May the Goddess be with you all, may she hold you high in your every hour of need.

Contents

Introduction

'Becoming Pagan' is simply a bite sized introduction to many aspects of Paganism, one cannot say all aspects, as Paganism today is huge and no list can be exhaustive.

The book aims to go back to basics, explaining things in the simplest of terms but not forgetting we are in the 21st century. Contents are based on common and weekly asked questions, by those Ty helps to teach and facilitate. It is not a 'one' way it is just 'a' way, to help anyone find their path.

There are eight chapters, corresponding to the eight spokes on the wheel of the year, most with three sub-chapters, introducing a great deal of areas and common features associated with Paganism, for example Tarot cards, witchcraft and meditation.

Accompanying the chapters on the sabbats will either be a prayer, a dedication or associated deity (mainly British or Northern European). There is a separate extensive chapter on deities - these are simply what Ty has researched. The book aims to look back in history and acknowledge our ancestors' ways, how they looked to nature even emulating it to learn and understand it, but more importantly how to survive. However, this book tries to retain the insight of a modern world, which can have a stark contrast to the Pagan faith, with its slow but apparent recognition in law and legislation of prisons and even pagan prisoners. It addresses life's equality and society's inequalities; it covers the stages of life and many of its values and attributes.

There are practice guides, suggested further reading and even a few exercises to help you apply your reading or new knowledge. These bite-sized chapters hope to provide starting platforms, genuine guidance from an experienced and empirical point of view, hopefully without opinion or bias. May 'Becoming Pagan' point you in a good direction and help you to find the answers to your individual questions, may it help you to understand your family member or loved-one's faith. May it assist you to become the Pagan you are or have desired to be, or simply be a definitive guide to your decision not to be a Pagan!

Interview with a Pagan

Having interviewed an atheist Pagan to get a general view, the results were fascinating. Robert clearly articulated deity is within himself, he and they are one. He does not 'externalise' his deity nor does he differentiate between the god and the goddess, they are all one.

He does not worship deity *per se*, as to worship is what monotheistic religions do – worshiping an external god is about penance and subservience. His internal recognition and acceptance of the divine is about reverence and recognition.

Robert does however partake in Pagan ritual, this often involving Pagans who do actually 'externalise' deities – even having a nominated person or persons playing the role of a god or goddess or invoking one. This, says Robert is a way to focus - it helps to embody the metaphor, helping him to focus upon a given deity. He further emphasises that there is no 'us and them' in reference to us humans and those gods and goddesses, although he does acknowledge they – deities – are more powerful.

Robert further adds to the above that working with other

Pagans of different paths with different methods is absolutely fine, it is all part of learning and tolerance. Not only recognising other paths within the faith, but respecting them and also learning from them.

Finally Robert adds that worship is about subservience and penance, inferiority and superiority and that is not what Paganism is, he quotes John Robinson's 'honest to God' who said (in reference to God) '...not a man with a beard in the sky, but God is within' (this is not necessarily an exact quote).

Finally he concludes with a smile and a quotation from 'Starhawk':

'...if that which you seek, you find not within yourself, you will never find it without.'

[From *Charge of the Goddess*].

1. WHEEL OF THE YEAR
The 8 Sabbats

Samhain / Sawhain

31ˢᵗ of October

Starting with Samhain, as this is the New Year to the Celts. Sometimes spelt Sa'hain, pronounced most frequently as Sow-ine, is the 31ˢᵗ of October, this is the old 'All Hallows eve', but of course the Pagan tradition undoubtedly precedes that. It is the time when the veil is thinnest between this world and the spirit world. Our Green Man (Herne the Hunter or the Horned God) goes into the woods at night to round up the lost souls and send them to their place of rest.

Pagans celebrate their past and their ancestors at this time of the year, the most important time to celebrate lost loved ones,

1

whether that was your pet cat recently deceased or your great grandmother, it is also in a modern world a time to celebrate with absent loved ones. At the time of feast we lay a table for the number of attendees to the meal and another place for absent friends, we toast and cheer to them as if they were present – because to Pagans when someone is gone or lost – they are not – they are still present in ones heart and in spirit. The Celts believed (like the Amazonian tribes and the Native Indian Americans) that wisdom and memory is carried in ones bones – in the DNA.

Celtic Pagans celebrate their New Year at this time and it is still common today for fellow Pagans to greet their Celtic family and friends – even if they do not live in Wales, Ireland or Scotland anymore – with a greeting of 'Happy New Year' or 'Blessing for the New Year'. November the first becomes New Year's Day.

This time of the year is the most abundant, with fruit on the trees and vegetables in the ground, berries and nuts, this is the time to feast, we begin to get fat for the winter and store our food and even fatten the live stock. White pears and pale plums are native to Britain as are damsons, it is also the time for apples (and Cider). Apples are the most sacred food to many Pagans as it is directly associated with the Goddess, and when cut it forms a pentacle (5 pointed star) and encompassed by the outer edge of the apple can be perceived as a Pentagram (5 pointed star encompassed in a full circle).

We light candles at this time of the year to draw the good spirits close and to keep the 'bad' or undesirable spirits away! This is where the pumpkin-lantern idea came from.

Witches have a particular affinity with the forest and often do a ritual for, or in, a forest – the alternative is to do a path finding exercise.

Samhain Prayer

Samhain is the time
The veil is thinnest upon this night
Of Celtic New Year
Only a fine mist is between
This world and the other
The other of spirit, and so
Our ancestors, our past loved ones.
Time now is to reflect to give thanks
And celebrate, celebrate
And welcome absent ones
As the dead do stir.

We sit to dine and we feast
This time of abundance, berries, fruits, nuts,
Root vegetables and ale or cider be.
A time we forget about the yearning
For our souls to be free
We lay extra spaces at the table
For those we once loved or knew
And invite them to dine

We ask for their wisdom
And give them gratitude
And endeavour to remember that
Which is sacred and true.
So remember to wash away the old
All energy that does not serve us any more
Invite in all those unreachable loved ones
Alive or dead
And welcome in the spirit, welcome in the New Year
With open heart and open door.

Winter Solstice/Yule

23rd of December

Yule and winter solstice come for us to celebrate the birth of the new light. The winter solstice, 21st December is the time of the longest night, thereafter the nights grow shorter and this is what we truly celebrate – the beginning of the end of the winter, although we have far to go through the winter into the light of Bridget at Imbolc. This would indeed have been a scary time of the year for our ancestors. Times would have been difficult, supplies short, days even shorter, the ancient land of Britain would have been covered in deep thick woodlands, a place quite formidable when full of bear, lynx, boar and wolf. So let us honour those amazing creatures who only reside now in our hearts or on lands far away.

The tree and boughs of evergreen represent hope, a continuation of the 'green' through the winter when so much dies, life and re-birth. Holly can directly represent the Holly King (an extension of the Green Man that once was the Green King). Holly King is the ruler of the first half of the year, the waxing half, he will fight once more at summer solstice and this time he will die and give way to the Oak King to rule the new, waning, first half of the year.

Baubles on the tree, that once were a candle or candles on the yule log represent light, a focus of hope, strength, warmth and the light that is to be re-born. The yule log would have had to come from the local land or as a gift, never purchased. The yule log would have to be a good size in order to burn for twelve days following Yule then extinguished and saved to light the yule log acquired that year to burn the following year. This represented a continuation of light, warmth and good fortune; the ashes would have been saved and traditionally the wood would have been ash or oak

The cylindrical quality also represents the sun. Later on oranges became a representation too, often spiked with cloves and given as a gift. Here you can see the Christian adaptation; they celebrate the birth of the Son (boy) we celebrate the birth of the Sun. There is good evidence Jesus was not born anywhere near to Yule or winter solstice, so much, with fervour, did the 'Pagans' celebrate this time of year, clinging with tenacity to the hope and light to get them through tough times, the Christians fixed Jesus' birth to coincide with our sun-birth. It is very clear now to those who have finally opened their eyes to see that Stonehenge is a place to celebrate the dead and the winter solstice.

Ivy as well as holly is an ancient traditional decoration for both inside and outside of the house, the doorways and windows and hearth. Some say the ivy is the feminine representation and holly the male (and there you have your balance). Mistletoe is of course sacred and traditionally represents fertility and good fortune, particularly revered by the Druids especially if found growing in oak (mistletoe grows in many trees, the sticky berries spread by birds, the mistletoe can literally grow from most branches). Holly is often referred to as a catcher of bad spirits and misfortune too – due to its prickly leaves. A strong definitive symbol of life and good fortune though.

Winter Solstice Prayer

We celebrate
Death
And rebirth
The longest night
Of the whole year
And yet
As the sun rises, thereafter,
A new day is borne, and the nights
Begin to wane
We celebrate with merriment and laughter.

We deck our homes and hearth
With holly and ivy
A picture in our hearts will suffice
And we can remember, the tales of the gathering of Yule logs
As we hug a radiator
And wade through postmodern fogs.
So embedded are tradition and images,
To be a part of it all
We need only
Close our eyes
And the hearth of the fire
Glowing in our hearts
And the ever-greenery
Protective all around
Will be no surprise.

HAIL to Yule
The darkness of winter solstice
To the re-birth of the sun
To protection and the tenacity of hope

As we plough through winter
With our own strategies, with which to cope.
Knowing how hard or cold or difficult
These times may be,
The Goddess is with us, keeping us warm, feeding us,
And setting us free

Imbolc

February 1st

This is the time to celebrate the coming of spring, the survival of winter and the birth of the new light. Often, in the old days, as today, Imbolc was celebrated at the time of the first sightings of snowdrops or a newborn lamb, in times of old this would be a difficult time of the year, with little to celebrate with other than oat cakes, dried or cured meat, maybe a few vegetables left from storage. Today we can only honour that harshness with twenty four hour shops, garages and street lights and sign posts to get us there. It is as important to us today as it was then so we can honour our ancestors and be grateful for our plenitude today. One of the great (Irish) goddesses that is invariably associated with Imbolc is Bridget sometimes referred to as Bride, from the Christianisation of Bridget into St. Bride or she is often known as Breed.

Bridget is the goddess of smiths and metalwork, therefore

goddess of the anvil – that which forges life from the earth from iron, which ties in with her being goddess of midwifery – actual birth, this then can be said to be re-birth, healing and therefore associated as goddess of springs and wells and a 'dressing' of a well in her name and honour is still widely practiced today. To the Pagan paths that practice the triple goddess aspect of 'Maiden, Mother, Crone' she is the maiden and usually depicted in flowing white.

One particular Imbolc ritual is to have a woman come into the room or ceremony dressed in black, to leave and return in either green or white – depicting the winter leaving and the coming of spring. Bridget is daughter to the Lord of Ireland – Dagda and sister to Ogham – the god of literature, her other brother is Don god of death and the journey to the heavens – usually known in Druidry as the 'blessed isles'. Don and Bridget can be seen as opposites but they are two integral, important and fundamental aspects of one whole, like the Ying and Yan.

Bridget is also goddess of healing, goddess of midwifery, actual birth and birth of creativity and therefore poetry. She travels the sky at Imbolc eve and bestows life and blessings upon the land on February first or second. You can call or invoke her or dedicate anything to Bridget anytime, not just at Imbolc.

Spring Equinox

March 21ˢᵗ

This time brings hope of sunshine and warmer weather, many smiles and improved health when it arrives. This is a precious time between Imbolc and Beltane often referred to as a 'lesser sabbat', but a beautiful time to celebrate and give thanks, a time to plant seeds and bulbs, to slough off the last dregs of winter. This is a traditional time to open all your doors and windows to let in the new spring air.

Already by now there should be daffodils and crocuses, first signs of bluebells, clematis and much more, it is time to put out the herbs, so carefully maintained over winter, with care in case there any more frosts. This is also time to sweep the patio or sort out the window boxes.

At this part of the wheel of year (metaphysically) the god or lord courts the goddess, becoming her consort, it is a time for Blodeuwedd (see below), Demeter, Eoster, the Holly King is in his prime. Night and day are now even once again, the clocks go back and the nights will begin to shrink, the days grow longer, very slowly.

Blodeuwedd is said to be the Welsh goddess of spring.

Blodeuwedd

Translated as lady of the flowers, or 'flower face', blodyn is flower in Welsh, blodau is flowers. Pronounced **Blod-ey-w-e** (as in errand) -**th** (but a hard short 'th') like weather.

9

There are slight variations on her story, the oldest book dates back to about the late 13th century, remember these stories, all of the Mabinogion, Taliesin etc, were written by Christian monks, and would have a Christian bias. Remember that there was no 'marriage' for example, weddings were simply the affirmation under an oak tree to declare you would spend one year and one day with someone, then you went back to the tree and decided if you wanted to spend longer with them or not! There was no 'adultery', infidelity male heir-ship and all that stuff that derives from a modern day wedding (which is literally law abiding and to commit an offence of the marriage is to break that law).

On that note, Arhianrod (goddess and lady 'of the silver wheel') declared that her son, Llew LLaw Gyffes, would never marry a mortal woman (owing to ill deeds he allegedly bestowed upon his mother). Her words were to the effect of 'never marry a woman of this world'. However, Math and Gwydion, Llew's cousins (some say uncles) were able to assist, Gwydion being the most powerful magician in the land, they made a wife for Llew.

They made a fair and beautiful woman from the sacred oak flowers, meadow sweet and broom, here alone you can see the elevation to goddess made from such beauty and sanctity. It was claimed she was more beautiful than any mortal woman, and when Llew made love to his new wife she became whole. Sadly it was soon when Llew Llaw Gyffes had to leave his home, his castle and his lovely new bride. Some say he went to war, some say he went to visit his family. However in his absence came a leader of an army (some would have you believe he was a dashing handsome knight), his name was Gronwr Pebyr (Lord of Penllyn), they both fell in love instantly and were together that very night (there is a Parallel her to the Norse story of Beowulf).

Gronwr Pebyr assumed position as her lover and head of the castle in Llew's absence, so in love were they, they plotted the death of her husband – Llew Llaw Gyffes, however there was only one way, a most unique and unusual way in which he could be killed. Naturally Llew was outraged upon his return to find Gronwr Pebyr in his place, but Blodeuwedd pacified him and took him into the woods, there she arranged for Llew to 'demonstrate' unto her the only unique way in which he could be killed. Upon the balance of the cauldron under a thatched roof with his back to a goat, Gronwr leaped from the woods by the river bank and pierced Llew with the required spear. Llew turned into an injured Eagle and managed to fly away, he was later found by his family and Gwydion returned him to human form and he was nurtured back to health, despite this being a lengthy process.

Blodeuwedd and Gronwyr lived together for that time, until Llew returned launching an assault on his castle, Blodeuwedd sought sanctuary in the forest by the river, there she was found and cast into an owl so she could never see the light of day again (or be seen).

The only way in which to kill Llew Law Gyffes was in a Cauldron (or bath) by a river bank beneath a thatched roof (so neither outside nor inside), whilst wrapped in a fishing net with his back to a goat (some say one foot on that goat!!) and one foot on the rim of the container of water (bath or Cauldron). Then pierced by a spear that took one year of Sundays to make, no sooner no longer, some further specify the time and the wood.

Beltane / Beltain

Beltane eve April 30th Beltane / May day – May 1st

After the passing of the spring equinox in which the nights and days balance and the lord is consort to the Goddess, he is now courting her, and the days get longer and the nights are shorter. The goddess is now or soon to be pregnant – metaphysically, as nature now is multiplying.

A time of fun and merriment in the woods, games for children, and in days of old (and still in rural areas), a time for young men and women to go into the woods and chase each other with the view to being a 'couple'. This is a time of fertility, and many Pagans perform fertility rituals, but not all, and invariable these are not the myths discussed in hush tones, but symbolically of the fertility of the goddess and of the lord / god / her consort.

This time of the year is when the goddess's belly is full of life symbolising and representing the busy life of nature, of the birds and the bees who are busy with their own ritual, pollinating, mating, laying and hatching of eggs.

This sabbat is glorious and full of body and abundance, although not crop time yet, far from it, there would simply be some be vegetables left over from winter, a few leeks or potatoes, leaves and shoots, maybe jams and chutneys, although today there is much abundance everday, however some Pagans still do follow the seasons as best as they can.

Beltane also pertains to fire, and many say the god of fire 'Bel'. Cattle were driven through fire hoops in the old days, this was

12

for two reasons – to purge the livestock of fleas and ticks, and to 'cleanse' them spiritually to bring fertility and abundance, pagans also 'leap' over a fire at Beltane for good luck, and even 'couples' leap together for fertility, synonymous with leaping over the broom at hands fasting.

Another tradition of at this time of the year was to light a fire on a hill top and once it was seen by a neighbouring village hill or farm then they would light another and so on. Other associations include May blossom (never to be brought into the home before May 1ˢᵗ), May Day and the May Queen as well as the coming of the light, purification and cleansing and therefore fire - the coming of the sun, the hope of sun and warmth.

Summer Solstice

June 21ˢᵗ
Summer Solstice, (Comhain – Wicca), Canol Haf - Welsh

This is the time of the longest day, the night is at its shortest, June 21ˢᵗ is the calendar date, and celebrations ensue from sunrise to sunset, and so the nights will begin to grow longer.

Many Pagans celebrate this by rising before dawn and drumming up the sun, solitary or in groups, groves of Druids, covens of witches.

Upon this day is the time of the battle between the Holly King and the Oak King, where the Oak King will win and the Holly

King will die. The Oak King then rules the second half of the year – the waning half.

We celebrate this time with images of the sun, a sun dial or sun wheel, often a mirror on our altar (some have one specifically for magical and altar purposes, but this is by no means essential), ribbons or any small items of golden coloured or yellow, or even red and orange to represent the fire, the burning of the sun, the candles. It is a time for herbs of fennel, arnica and sunflowers, calendula officialise – British marigolds, the only ones edible.

We adorn our altars with cloths of red and yellow, decorating with flowers, a simple vase with a few yellow or red and orange flowers can be sufficient.

Remember, in Norse and Hindu and other traditions the Sun is female, not male, but we can celebrate the same qualities here only from a nurturing perspective rather than a tenacious 'warrior' like energy.

Hail to the Coming Sun

Hail to the coming sun
To the longest day
When the sun shines longer
And the night shrinks away

Hail to the coming of the sun
To strength and abundance
To renewing of the sprit
Spirit of self
And spirits of the land

A time to rejoice
To bare the skin to the air

To give our worries to the river
To walk without a care

A time of sunflowers for our wisdom
Sun rays for nutrients
Long green grass
Flowers and full bloom trees
For our spiritual nourishment, as well as that of our bodies.

Hail to the coming of the sun
As we thank the goddess
For this strength, this direction
Our food and water blessed
By the divine masculine and golden light
Hail to the coming sun, *we* are blessed.

Lammas / Lughnasa

August 1st

Celebration of the crops and corn, honouring the Corn God and the Sun God (Llugh is Irish, Llew is the Welsh equivalent). This is a time to separate the wheat from the chaff and as always what we see in nature our ancestors emulated, and so today we may not be involved directly with the crops and wheat fields, but we can meet the Corn God (by ritual, evocation or a simple journey or meditation) and we can address our own chaff and get rid of what is no longer needed in our lives. This could be half a wardrobe of clothes donated to charity, or it could be getting rid of doubt or a fear.

This is a time to separate what has been gained or achieved and at the same time what is no longer required. It is about the sun and long days, also for some Pagans, it is about death and eradication, even about ancestors – how they would have slaved away twelve to fourteen hours a day to cut wheat by hand often in blazing sun, to ensure their families and communities had flour for bread for the coming winter. The Christians adapted their loaf mass from Lammas celebrating the bread as the body of Christ; however to Pagans the bread is the embodiment of the earth and thus both the God and the Goddess.

Why not try making a loaf from scratch? It is easier than you think, throw in a spoonful of honey to represent the Goddess and a spoon full of fennel seeds to represent the God, it is delicious. This could be your 'giving up' (like an offering); giving up your time to learn how to bake and then another two hours to make the loaf (one hour is putting your feet up to have a cup of tea while it is rising!)

See further reading for an amazing easy to follow bread book, with a great guide to making bread from scratch, by hand or in a machine for you modern Pagans.

Ode to Lugnasa

Hail to the Summer Sun
Hail the long days of wheat
The olden days of toil and sweat
Now we only celebrate
With the grass beneath our feet.
Today the bread is oh so ready made
And we can give up our work
For a few days
And sit and picnic under a tree'
Or in the shade.
So let us spare a thought for those
Who have passed us by,
The old ones, who worried for the days
Of winter and hunger ahead.
Now we have shops and bread
In abundance instead.
Let us hail the Corn King
And offer him our troubles;
Offer him all we do not need
And measure the achievements gained.
And think of the corn and barley
What can we give to them?
What song can we sing?
To praise the Sun and corn and barley fields
What can we let go of?
What can the glory of the Sun
to us bring?

Autumn Equinox

21st, 22nd or 23rd September

Personally I like to do a pilgrimage at this time; I seem to be unique in this; although many a Pagan pontificates about a pilgrimage. It does not have to mean walking to Spain or to a cathedral in France (you can if you want to!). It can be as simple as walking up a mountain, walking in the forest – just go a bit further or walk a bit longer than normal, try talking a picnic or take a friend, celebrating can be as humble as a sandwich by a tree, it is your intent that counts, your heart and reverence for the next spoke on the wheel of the year. It does not have to be all about huge rituals, but of course it can be if you wish. There are an increasing amount of open rituals now, see networking chapter for further details.

Equinox is of course about balance, of both night and day at equal length on or around the 21st September the nights will lengthen after this time of balance. This is a great time to seek the balance within, I recommend scales on your altar or just bring your baking or weighing scales out on to a shelf in the kitchen (or put it on your altar if you are not baking for a day or two).

Print or, better still, draw a picture of a set of scales and put it on your altar or any wall you fancy.

When I dance I like to take two pieces of drift wood and two two-pence coins with me for the altar. Then, with these I make my own scales, pennies and two pence's are made of copper and really good for grounding. Balance can be about wealth too and having enough 'pennies' to get you through the winter.

Autumn Equinox is an abundance of fruit, pears, apples and berries although they are coming to an end now, it is time for damson, chutneys, pickles and jam. As usual our ancestors would have looked to nature to emulate it; to learn how to survive. They would see the last of the fruit on the trees, the squirrels busy burying their nuts, birds flying south, bears preparing to hibernate, bees and bugs would begin to disappear. A tangible taste is in the air, the days get cooler quicker in the afternoons, the nights are earlier and earlier each day, the mornings will soon begin to get darker. You may even begin to feel more sleepy soon, although it is still six weeks to Samhain, much feasting and work is yet to be done before our ancestors could afford to slow down and go into dream time.

As this is a time of balance it is also a time of healing, according to Kate West this time of the year, in the old days, would have been a time to release prisoners. Prisoners were very rarely taken in old battles, as it was costly to feed them, so those taken would have been of rank and importance, keeping them and releasing them at this time of the year ensured they would have less mouths to feed and it was a good bargaining chip to possibly get their friends and family back, and this meant more labourers to fetch the last of the food and wood and preparations for the coming winter.

Also this time of the year can be very wet and windy, making roads impassable in the days of old, so you begin to stay home and settle in, you would not journey far or start a battle or feud. A great time to reflect on putting your grudges out to air, to repay debt (that could be words said in the heat of the moment you may regret), it could be an unpaid bill or an emotion you have been wanting to tell someone about, now is the time to balance, to heal, to set free your own 'prisoners'.

Suggestions:

Seek the balance of your life – in your relationships – is there equal give and take?

Your diet – is there equal good food, fibre and not much sugar, salt and rubbish? (although a little soul food should not be missed I say).

How is your sleep? Is there equal balance of dream sleep and meditation? Or sleep and exercise?

Do some writing, keep a journal or even write a chart with positive and negative (or write 'not so positive' if you do not want to use the 'negative' word).

Keep it simple and it will be fun not a chore.

2. INITIATION, OR NOT?

Traditionally Paganism is not an initiatory faith (I am reluctant to use the word religion), however in a modern society, in Britain, Pagan is the legally recognised umbrella term for many paths including Wicca and witchcraft, the later in all its diversities and glory, a select few can be seen further on. It is not uncommon in many witchcraft and Wicca paths for self initiation, and many adults in paganism in general often have a naming ceremony or just a blessing.

Traditionally there is a 'rite' of passage in witchcraft – into a coven and into a grove for Druids. Usually what 'goes on in a coven, stays in the coven', and you are sworn to secrecy. So any initiation would be top secret. The great rite is no longer a complete secret – at least as to what it is.

To quote Peter Nash:

'.. but unless you are part of a coven or similar you may never know what the initiation is, suffice to say you should never be forced into something you clearly do not want to do.'

Personally I was terrified when I first started to learn about

Paganism, the practise thereof anyway, with my Judeo-Christian background I thought all religions had some form of initiation and witchcraft probably involved flogging and intimacy (or worse). I have no idea where I got these notions from but well over twenty years ago in a small part of Wales dominated by dogma for hundreds of years, it was probably palpable from the air one breathed.

Having started to find my own books on witchcraft and discovering this marvellous path of 'hedge' witchcraft I felt no initiation was required, and then I discovered the option (or opportunity) of self initiation. I grasped it with gusto, thinking, in my naivety, if I initiated myself no one else would need to. And that was what I did, as scared as I was it was a basic yet moving and beautiful experience, but today it is still not essential. There are priests and priestesses who do a full initiation to any Pagans of any age, gender, nationality, sexual preference or background, if that is really what you would like, however initiations are not allowed in British prisons.

Choosing your lord and lady (or not)

There are no hard and fast rules of choosing, it should come from the heart and there are no time constraints. For example Celtic, Egyptian, Norse (Asatru) are but a few of the pantheons you can chose from. Feel how they resonate with you, always go with it if a particular path feels familiar or you take a particular interest in it, you can do this as often as you wish, even mixing deities or paths.

The idea of the Lord and Lady is a focal point for worship and meditating, to help with focus and understanding in ones life – no matter what situation we find ourselves in or what our upbringing was. The Lord and Lady are aspects of the Goddess and it helps us to break down the vast incredible awesomeness of the One Goddess, often referred to as Gaia or Mother Earth.

The Lord and the Lady are equal male and female energy; forging a balance, as nature must, and we are worshipers of that nature. The Lord and Lady or a god and goddess can be a centre and focal point for your altar. Some pagans have a large or expensive statue of the chosen deity (or deities), but again it is not necessary, a dried flower, an apple, feather or twig will suffice. Always learn as much as you can about a chosen deity if you are going to work with that energy or do a dedication or ritual. Your time and your energy can be the modern day equivalent of 'sacrifice', and show your dedication to this deity.

Another option is to have one or two plain figures and adorn them with various gifts, different coloured ribbon for example. This is my personal favourite; I have a large neutral statue that is feminine in appearance, as I have two 'ladies', my primary worship are both Ma'at and Kerridwen, for my personal reasons. So I have a 'neutral' goddess-like figurine (about 18 inches tall) and I drape various ribbons and cords about her, the colours of which are associated with times of the year. I give her a gift of a golden coloured jewelled mirror as a representation of the God and of the Son or Sun, (it cost me £2.99 from a gift store). Many years later (now), I have small off-shoot altars, one of which is a mini Egyptian altar and there I place gifts and mini statues with whatever or whomever I am working with at any time. This has taken me a long tome to establish, there is no rush.

3. DEITIES

Welsh / Celtic Gods and Goddesses

These are the most popular, with fairly readily available information in textbooks, particularly the Mabinogion or correctly pronounced and in Welsh – the Mabinogioau.

Goddesses

Kerridwen (or Cerridwen)
Mother and crone figure. Goddess of hearth/home/kitchen/cauldron, maker of the elixir of life for son Avagddu / Afagddu (ugly one).

Blodeuwedd
The flower goddess, Llew Llaw Gyffes' wife, made from flowers for his mother (Arhianrhod), placed a curse upon him that he shall never have a mortal wife (Mabinogion). She is depicted as maiden, is associated with owls and true love, devotion and

beauty, she is a goddess of the spring made from meadowsweet, broom and the flowers of oak.

Arhianrhod *(means 'Silver Wheel' in Welsh)* pronounced ar-y anne rhod (like rod but you need to roll the 'r' over the top of your tongue). She took second place as virgin* to a great king and warrior who was only allowed to place his feet in a virgin's lap when not in battle. To prove herself worthy, Arhianrhod had to step over a magical rod, but this showed she was no virgin and gave birth to twins, one of whom was Dylan.

Rhiannon formidable goddess, powerful, associated with grace and the white horse. Often referred to as a 'queen' and often a goddess of the 'other world', first wife to Pwyll, King of Dyfed then to Manawyddan – the Welsh sea god, her story is an incredible one from the realm of the gods to the mortal earth to false punishment, loss and finding of her son, Pryderi.
* Previous/original meaning to 'virgin' was an unmarried woman of great benevolence.

Gods

Cernunnos (Kern-unn-oss) sometimes referred to as generic, European or Continental, he is the god that sits with horns on his head, a ram-headed serpent in one hand and a torc (Celtic necklace of status) in the other hand. In fairly modern Paganism he seems to be associated with the Horned God – the Green Man or Herne the Hunter (god of the woods, the forest, animals, nature)

Manawyddan – Sometimes referred to as Welsh Sea God or God of the ocean., second husband to Rhiannon

Llew or Lleu – (Welsh equivalent to the Irish Lugh) the Sun God, represents harvest, Lammas (Lughnasa), the Sun, heat and strength.

Dylan – also a Welsh god of the sea as when he was born he leaped from the arms of his mother (Arhianrhod) and dived into the sea to swim as well as any fish, and no wave was able to slow him.

Arawn – God or King of the Annwn – the Celtic otherworld, son to Don – Welsh Mother Goddess. He fought the 'battle of the trees'.

Amathaon – God of Agriculture also son to Don, also a magician who taught his brother the craft (Gwydion). It is said it was he who was the cause of 'battle of the trees' due to a theft (see Mabinogion for all full stories of these gods and more).

The Green Man

Formerly known as the Green King (and is still so in many Pagan minds and ideals).

Historical rumour has it that the green 'king' was demoted so not to offend any other king – especially after 1066 and the Norman conquest, nothing was better or took the title of King other than the King of England (and therefore Scotland, France and Ireland), Wales only comes into the King's realm periodically through history, not all of it.

On midsummer's day the Holly King dies and the Oak King prevails and wins – many a local tradition then say he goes on to meet and marry the 'May Queen', undoubtedly a modern day aspect of the Goddess. The Oak King rules the second half – the waning half of the year from mid summer to mid winter (the solstices).

At Winter Solstice the Holly King rises, fights the Oak King and he wins, serving as King of the first and waxing half of the year, midwinter to midsummer.

The Green Man or Green King are also known as the man of the woods or the forest, incarnated in the form of Herne the Hunter. The lord or male aspect to Pagan worship in general can be simply followed by the wheel of the year.

At the time of Imbolc the crone winter Goddess is reborn into the fair maiden at Imbolc after which, at the time of Spring Equinox, the lord aspect emerges as consort and courts the goddess, then making her pregnant at Beltane (hence the great fertility of Beltane).

The Lord then is re-born as son to the Goddess at Winter Solstice when he is born as son or sun when the new light returns. The lord is in many ways second to the Goddess, but by no means less important, undermined or undervalued in any way. There are indeed many Pagans that follow the path of the Goddess – going so far as to believe she can exist without any masculine aspect (and even have their own feminist creation theory), but to most Pagans there can not be one without the other. Nature can not exist without balance, we need Ying (feminine) and Yan (masculine) to harmonise, to procreate, to fertilise, for life to continue. The 'Lord' or 'God' aspect is a powerful and fundamental part of the Pagan creation myth too. To the Goddess he is consort, lover, son and this is a never ending cycle throughout the wheel of the year. He supports and nurtures her, he loves and honours her. They co-exist.

In a coven – frequently – the male is the priest and stands before or even beneath the 'ruler' of a coven. That ruler is the priestess – the representation of the Goddess (unless sexuality dictates otherwise, not all covens are heterosexual, female only or an even mix of male and female).

Norse Tradition Gods & Goddesses

In the beginning there were Giants and to cut a long story short Odin led his brothers to slay Ymir – the first Giant and somewhat ruler of the Giants, the Giants would have fled in fear, but drowned swiftly in Ymir's blood, Odin used Ymir's giant body to create many parts of the now known Universe.

See the Norse Creation Myth for full details.

Odin (pronounced Wodin or Wotin) became the 'father' of the gods whose partner (some say wife, but 'marriage' was totally different then to what it is now) Frigg bore a son called...

Balder (or Baldur) the Sun God, God of Goodness and Wisdom. Odin hung from the Asatru tree of life – the great ash-tree of the universe this is known as:

Yggdrasil from which Odin hung for a number of nights and days, most likely 9 (the sacred number known to the Norse) in which time he was given the gift of the knowledge of the runes. Odin sent out his 2 ravens to bring back news of all that was happening in the world, the middle world known as Midgard, world of men, mortals.

Frey God of Nature, Peace and Prosperity, his sister is:

Freya Goddess of Nature, fertility, beauty and love, both are twin offspring to Niord.

Asgard home of the gods

Hel Queen of the Dead or Goddess of the Underworld, not a place of punishment like modern society depicts – 'Hel' was an honourable and welcoming place with vestal virgins, flowing mead and great feasting.

Loki known as the trickster with a reputation as God of Keyholes and Doorways, but also God of Fire.

Nanna goddess and wife to Balder (see above).

Scoll the wolf who persued the Sun.

Hati the wolf who pursued the Moon.

Ran Goddess of the Deep Sea and 'wife' of

Aegir God of the Deep Ocean (they had 9 daughters – the '**Undines**').

Thor god of thunder – famed for his hammer – often the Norse symbol to many modern Pagans, in the old days he was truly a god for the working class, defender and protector of Paganism and of the people – unlike his father Odin who was really defender and warrior of the 'aristocracy' of the day. Thor is a very popular god, a most gentle giant, but with a wrath to draw down lightning. Some scholars say his hammer was used to break up the ice of the winter to help bring in the spring. His hammer is symbolic of the anvil and the smith as well as a symbol for fertility.

Tyr God of War, who sacrificed his hand to the wolf; use Tyr for protection.

Valhall (often pronounced 'Val-hal-a') this is where the dead warriors feasted.

Vidar (or Vali) – the silent God (from strength), kills many, he is both a god and Odin's other son, his mother is Odin's lover/mistress **Rind**.

Norse Deities continued

Norns the three fates:

Ur (or Wyrd) – past – or destiny
Verdandi - present, or 'necessity', who weaves the web of fate
Skuld – future or 'being' who tore this web

Together they are known as the Wyrd Sisters, who shape every single living human form, including humans, elves, the Giants and even the Gods. Sometimes the 'wyrd' is referred to as a single deity.

The 3 sisters could possibly be a 'mirror' or a platform upon which modern Pagans and Wicca take the idea or concept of the maiden, mother, crone aspect.

The 3 sisters can be seen with all their associations in the rune Peorth

According to Nigel Jackson medieval German midwives wove three different coloured cords together – red, black and white, at the birth of a baby, as a token for the new baby's future and a talisman for 'good wyrd', as in 'good luck' or good fate.

Sunna the Sun Goddess, remember the sun is feminine in the old Norse or Germanic tradition, unlike the Celtic or Northern European where the Sun is masculine. She is depicted as Sol in the rune cards; she is associated with mistletoe, the sacred plant, depicting the continued spirit of human life. Jackson further states that the Gods gave birth to the mistletoe when struck by lightning (and did not burn), this is synonymous with the Druid tradition whereby, still today, the sacred ceremony is held to cut down the sacred mistletoe (when found growing on oak) and this is done with a sickle. In old tradition and text it is said a Druid ought to cut the mistletoe with a golden sickle, now people are saying the gold comes from the Sun – reflecting off the metal. This all ties in very nicely together.

Heimedall (or Heimdahl) this is shown in the rune card Algiz, possibly associated with the Vanir – a race of gods and goddesses that represented fertility and protection (this included Frey and Freya).

Guardian of the Bifrost the rainbow bridge from Earth to the home of the Gods, Asgard. God, son of nine virgins, and associated with the ocean (the nine virgins are associated with nine waves, the 'ninth' wave is always used in magic or if sea water is to be collected for magical use).

Egyptian Gods and Goddesses

Atum early and ancient god – associated with creation and the creator, Serpent God. Later associated with the Sun, 'limits of the sky' and with Thebes. In ancient writing dates back to the 11th dynasty, later he was given more associations, for example connected to not just the Sun but the God of Sun Re (Ra). He is one of the top 8 most written about gods. He is totality, all that ends and all that begins, he comes from 'before all other gods', from the cosmic chaos, he was not made or born, he 'appeared', later using his bodily fluid (which ones vary) to create other gods, he created Shu and Tefnut, parents to Nut (see page 35).

Amun is also one of the top 8 most written about gods referred to as 'Amun, pre eminent'. Not until after the Thebian king of the new and middle kingdoms, was he re-invented as Amun-Re, he is associated with Mut (his consort) and Khasu the Moon (or lunar) God. He continued to be worshipped, through and into the 18th dynasty, where hymns were also made for him and to him.

Horus associated with wind and soaring high like the falcon, an 'avian' deity, some texts refer to him however as having the wings of a hawk, suffice to say he is portrayed with the head of a bird. This sky association also connects him the Sun and he has been found as early as 3,000 B.C. inside temples with 'hawk' wings and feathers and a sun disk, directly depicting him as a solar god. Some say one eye was the Moon the other the Sun and it was the Sun eye that was removed hence the 'all seeing eye' of Horus which is protective, protector of everything.

Imhotep a very high official of a king, said to be born a commoner, but due to his service to King Djoser, his vision and plans for the first pyramid left him patron saint of many things. He was a master at sculpting; he constructed the very first pyramid at Saqqara. He was later deemed the son of Ptah of Memphis. He further became associated with medicine. Further to this the Greeks associated him with healing, and to their god Asklepios. He is sculpted and depicted as a 'human' with an enlarged head or smooth surfaced hat (no hair), and nothing on top – for he is not a true god, but many images see him carrying the ankh.

Osiris - one of the most famous or infamous of the Gods. Husband to Isis the great Goddess of Magic. Osiris was ruler of Egypt; some say the original sun god, ruler of all Egypt. But Seth was extremely jealous of him, his rule, kingdom and wife (Isis), so Seth murdered him, and cut him up into 14 pieces and scattered him all over Egypt. Horus his son (with Isis) and Isis herself set about vengeance, and Isis went to collect all the pieces, she found them all except his phallus, but she made another one from magic, then made love to him and became pregnant. Isis built a temple for him. As he was not fully human, he was partly magic, he was banished to the underworld. There he became ruler and worked with Ma'at to judge those after body death because the Egyptians believed unequivocally in the afterlife, the body was merely a shell that housed the spirit of 'Ka', they continued on their 'journey' after the body dies.

Astarte - the western counterpart to Ishtar worshiped in Mesopotamia, (known as Inanna in Sumerian), a dual goddess of both love (and fertility) and of war, often reputed as a formidable (not to be messed with) goddess. Frequently associated with horses and chariots (which were used in Egyptian warfare). She is also said to have worn bull horns on her crown or helmet (a sign of strength, fertility, earth and domination).

Hathor wife of Horus, one of the oldest and most important goddesses. Often referred to as the Cow Goddess or Mother Goddess, she dates back to the pre-dynastic age. She is written about in both coffin text and pyramid text – in which she is associated with the sky, she is daughter of the Sun God Re, and is often seen coming out of reeds with the cow horn on her head (or cow ears) and the sun disk on her head (representing her father). She is invaluable to a lot of modern Pagans, Wiccans and witches in Britain and Europe today as she is further known as the Goddess of Joy, love, music, and even further associated with nature, fertility, music; even healer and protector.

Isis The Great Goddess of Magic, wife to Osiris (also reported to be brother and sister) who collects his body parts after he was murdered and dismembered. Vast numbers of temples were erected or named in her honour worldwide. The fellowship of Isis in Ireland attracts Pagan women from all over the world. She is famed in imagery for her wings – the wings of Isis, however she often wears the sun disk and cow horns upon her head. She was given special magical powers by the Sun God (Re) who secretly bestowed a magical name upon her (most witches today, even some Pagans who perform the slightest of magic or spells also have a 'secret' 'magic' name, it is often a part of initiation).

Ma'at Goddess of Justice and Truth is depicted in all the halls of justices and the weighing scales of life is her symbol, upon which the heart of the dead is placed, and on the other side of the scales is a feather, an ostrich feather is also displayed upon her crown. If the heart of the deceased is lighter or the same as that of the feather then they are worthy to enter the otherworld, having lived a good honest life. As with many of the above gods, their temples are in Karnak, hers in the precinct of Montu temple. She is associated with balance, order, divine order and harmony. She restores the balance of the cosmos by using her hand to stop injustice and her feather to judge, she is sometimes referred to as the Goddess of Love – in the cosmic sense. Ma'at is known to date back to the beginning of Egypt, to the order of things, to the creation, she is counterpart to chaos.

Nut daughter of Shu (air) and Tefnut (moisture – or dew) – the elements that created Nut and her brother Geb (the Earth god), before there was anything else on Earth. *Note here the Earth god is male and sky goddess female. In many other cultures we find Mother Earth and Father Sky.* Nut is depicted naked leaning over her brother with her hands and feet placed in all 4 cardinal directions, north, south east and west. She is sometimes seen as a celestial cow, she is mother to Osiris, Isis, Seth and Nephthys. Some say Nut's laughter is the thunder and her tears are the rain. She is associated with the stars and Milky Way, she is also associated with the sun rise at winter solstice.

Bastet the Cat Goddess, daughter of Re the Sun God, originally a lioness who was able to inspire terror. The temple of Bastet is now only fallen red blocks (the main culture was in Baubastis in the Egyptian Delta), and the original temples housed sacred cats. Bastet had a rather scary, formidable almost terrifying aspect at the beginning of her reign (lions can kill and will eat humans!). Over the dynasties her temperament pacified, she became more cat like (we would say domestic now) so that she would kill or chase away vermin and so she soon became more mother like. Kittens do need a lot of attention and so her developed and enhanced personality soon became a symbol of motherhood and she became the protector of pregnant women. The Greeks associated her with their goddess Artemis.

Sekmet wife or consort of Ptah and daughter of the Sun God Re. A leonine goddess (lioness), Goddess of Danger and Destruction and also healing and protection, manifestation of the 'Eye of Ra' (and associated with Hathor). Patroness of battle (said to breath fire) she had the power to ward off pestilence, So powerful was she, with the ability to kill off so many humans poor Re, her father, feared there would be no one left to worship him.

Re thought the humans were plotting against him and sent his daughter to punish them, but in fear of the loss of all humans, with no one left to care for the land and the temples, he filled a lake with beer and dyed it red (ochre), and Sekmet assumed it was blood and drank to intoxication. The god sated, humanity was saved. Because Sekmet was so feared, the humans assumed she could ward off diseases and plagues that physicians could not. Hundreds of statues, seated and standing, of Sekmet were erected in the Temple of the Sun in honour of her father. A great statue of granite (as a lion-headed female human) is to be found in the Cairo Museum in Egypt.

Anubis the jackal god – often seen as a male human with a jackal head, occasionally a full (though still human-like) jackal, and frequently but not always with a tail. Both the tail and the blackness of the face of Horus is like a real jackal. The tail is club-like and more closely resembles one from a wolf or fox; his snout resembles a dog's. A jackal's hide is also brown not black. However as Horus represents death – as he presides over the dead his black colouring shows he is both the colour of the fertile soil and the colour of purification of the body after death (and mummification). He initially mummified Osiris when he died and was primarily there to care for the dead king, but later came to be associated with all of the dead and connected with most items of funerary.

He is known for and often shown as performing the 'opening of the mouth' ceremony – a ceremony where the attributes of life are given to the dead body to carry over into the next life.

He is seen with his dog-like ears erect and he wears a kind

of collar or ceremonial neck-piece. He is further referred to as guardian of graveyards.

Anubis is associated with Osiris (the first or original god and therefore his death etc), with Isis as he presided over her giving birth, with Ma'at and the scales of justice (he helped or even performed the weighting of the heart) and therefore Osiris again as lord of the underworld. He is found in most if not all pyramids, coffins and texts. It is said priests who performed ceremonies of the dead (mummification, opening of the mouth etc) wore a mask of Anubis.

Sobeck a crocodile god, he is an actual crocodile, shown as thus, not a human person with a crocodile head. His kind resided in the Nile and were seen as guardians and protectors of the sacred waters of the Nile that naturally flooded annually to irrigate the crops. One text writes he was 'taker of wives from husbands' at will so association with him gave both procreative and vegative fertility and is linked to cults of other gods like Osiris, Amun and the Sun God, the later giving us a Sobek-Re, making the Greeks associate him with their sun god Helios.

Nephthys sister to Isis, but she played a smaller roll than her sister; like Isis she is daughter to Nut and Geb. Her name translates as 'Mistress of the Mansion' or 'Mistress of the Enclosure'. It is reported that Nephthys had a son with Osiris – resulting in Anubis, some text also say Nephthys grieved considerably when Osiris was murdered by Seth and helped Isis to find his body parts (there so many variations on this). It is also reported that Nephthys was counterpart or even consort to Seth. That does mix a lot of brothers and sisters and brother and sister-in-laws.

Serpent Gods

Wadjet awesome cobra goddess, associated with green, perhaps a reference to her environment in Lower Egypt, the word 'Wajet' means 'to be green', she is countepart to the Goddess Neckbet. She became known as 'mistress of fear' or 'mistress of awe'. She is shown as an erect cobra ready to strike, her major cult centre was in 'the region of the ancient towns...' Later Buto, now Tell el-Fora, in the North West Delta. Per – nu ('house of fame') is the name of her temple. A period of time showed Sarcophagi and coffins made from her shape and later her image continues to be connected to funerary goods. The erect serpent is seen upon the crown of the Pharaoh. Sometimes Wadjet is shown upon the image statue of Sekmet or the 'Eye of Re'.

And also **Neckbet** – the vulture goddess I have to put her here as she is counterpart to Wadjet although she is a vulture goddess not a serpent goddess. She together with Wadjet are often referred to as the 'Two Ladies', often shown together as the cobra and vulture in partnership with the king's or pharoah's crown. The main deity of Upper Egypt sometimes seen as wearing the white crown of upper Egypt, as many other goddesses (above), she is sometimes referred to as the white cow (associating her in the ancient text with the Mother Goddess). She is sometimes shown in serpent form – the same as Wadjet.

Thoth deemed the God of Scribes (or of writers writing today), this came about as it was said he gave the knowledge and power of the hieroglyphs to humanity as a gift, as instructed by Re. It was the privileged few that were able to read and write. He was seen as guardian or overseer of those who could write the hieroglyphs, and read text. He is seen as an ibis or baboon – more frequently an ibis; the ibis beak is curved like a half moon. He is shown as a human male with the head of an ibis or as a full bodied baboon. He was seen as a Moon God in the beginning before he became god of writing. The hieroglyphs are also said to be the 'god's words'. Ashmunein (formerly known as Hermopolis) is the centre for his cult with a great many mummified baboons and ibis in the nearby cemetery. He is further associated and even at one point joined with Re, occasionally a baboon is shown with both the crescent moon and the sun disk upon his head. He was deemed a messenger and of great importance as he was the 'go between' betwixt the gods and the humans.

Apophasis deity of death and the underworld, deemed indestructible. Nothing can kill him, but he can be charmed or rendered temporarily disabled – shown frequently as the serpent and having his head chopped off by the great cat Re – the Sun God. His serpent body is said to be extremely long (50 feet or more). He is the great adversary of the Sun God Re and the embodiment of the power of dissolution, darkness, and non-being. It is said he had a great terrifying roar, he came from the empty dark chaos in the time before all creation. He is frequently associated with Seth and of course, Re. Apophasis is said to mesmerise all those on the barque of Osiris (the death boat that travels the underworld in the absence of the sun.

Apophasis is associated with all darkness, unexpected and sudden nocturnal events, this included storms, earthquakes and much more. Various spells were created to protect the people from this mighty snake, that is how we ended up with the Book of Horus – filled with all kinds of spells and protections, and various ways to protect against the 'evil' darkness. For example making a wax effigy (a look-a-like figure similar to that used in voodoo), then every morning chopping it up and melting or burning it (as in the paintings showing Re, the giant cat beheading Apophasis the snake). Another way is to draw a snake upon papyrus, put in a box, spit on it and set it on fire.

Conclusion

This draws one to think why bother? Why all that hassle? If we did not have opposition, threats and counterparts to love light and peace we could not measure the goodness and compassion. By having the likes of Horus (or Taran or Kali etc) we can know and understand balance, harmony, expanding our awareness and cosmic understanding, giving sense to our existence. This maybe one of the reasons Paganism has never died, we do not fear death, we take ancient tales thousands of years old and apply them to our everyday lives, we do not take them literally but metaphorically. We learn and have no need to lie or fear death (this is of course not necessarily automatic in Paganism, but can be found).

Selection of Paths:

Pagan (general)

Celtic Pagan those who tend to follow the path of the Celts and the ancestors that came to Britain approximately 500 BCE and the worship of the Gods and Goddess they brought with them, this can then be Welsh, Scottish or Irish Celtic or a combination thereof.

Anglo Saxon Pagan worship of Gods and Goddess and following of traditions from what once was Anglo Saxon country (now England) for example the formidable Black Annis from Leicestershire.

Picts, or Scottish Pagan followers of the formidable warriors from the north of the borders.

Cornish Pagan usually Pagans that are born in Cornwall or feel connected to it, they tend to be (like the Welsh) fiercely patriotic. People still do speak Cornish.

Egyptian Pagan those who follow an Egyptian path with Egyptian deities etc there are so many books on the subject, there are even books available on the ancient Egyptian language, hieroglyphs and deciphering them, and there are books on Egyptian ritual.

Eclectic many paths or a selection of parts from many paths and pantheons.

Druid

Witchcraft
- **Traditional**
- **Alexandrian**

- **Gardnerian**
- **Hedge**
- **Hereditary**
- **Georgian**
- **Wicca / Modern** (although there is a counter-argument that 'Wicca' is very old).

Heathen

Asatru / Norse / Odinist

Shaman

Pagans with Oriental Associations like I Ching or Chi Quong.

Gay Pagan

Atheist Pagan

Any combination i.e. Wicca Druid, Hedge Witch on a Druidic Path

This list is not exhaustive.

Deity-worshipping and Atheist Pagans

Over time I have discovered three shiny new types of Pagan (they may indeed not be regarded by some as shiny or new), these are:
- Those who internalise their deity
- Those who eliminate deity altogether believing in and worshiping the Goddess alone – as one whole.
- Those who have simply not decided if or what they will worship.
- Bringing us to a fourth category of agnostic Pagans –

those who believe in something but are not sure, yet, as to what.

• Finally there are also atheist and agnostic Druids (very few and far between, which may be contested in Druid circles). These few tend to procrastinate over the importance of ancestors, bloodline and the land, ancestors being much more important than (even completely superseding) deity, and the importance of worship and honouring our past leaves deity wanting or lacking in significance.

4. MEDITATION

The simplest way is to sit in a quiet and comfortable position – on your bed is fine but do not lay down until or if you intend to fall asleep, just sit and 'be'.

From here you can either visualise a dot on the wall or a picture or place an object in view like a flower – something that pleases your vision like a picture of the ocean, waterfall or sunset. Do not use photographs if they contain people, as this will invoke memories and emotions.

From here you can also visualise a candle (if safe to do so) or smoke from a joss stick / incense burner.

Try to blank your mind and then just 'see' what you see in front of you and think only of this item, if your mind wanders off, do not chastise yourself, just take a deep breath – in through the nostrils and out through the mouth and start again. If you can only do this for 30 seconds to start with – persevere and the length of time you can concentrate will grow.

Another excellent way to meditate is to sing, or hum a tune

over and over again alternatively, like many other traditions you could try a chant or mantra. This can be as simple as 'Hail to the Goddess provider of life, I am your son (or daughter), hail to the God I am your son (or daughter). You can make it as long or as short, as simple or as complex as you wish. The repetition of the sound will have a healing and balancing effect. Do not try to make it too long or too complicated however – unless you want to write a song or ballad.

Here is an example for a morning focus, as soon as you are up (this is a great time as you have just emerged from dream sleep and are just between realms), you should need very little time to relax and get into meditation 'mode'.

Recite 'Morning to the north, Morning Goddess and the Earth that sustains me. Morning to the east and the rising sun, thank you for a new day. Morning to the south, lord of fire and the breath of passion and motivation. Morning to the west and the waters of life.'

Maybe it can give you a springboard to write your own, remember these things need to be repeated (ideally daily) to be effective.

With tarot and oracle cards the simplest meditation is to sit there and stare at a card, write down what comes into your mind – no matter how silly or irrelevant it may seem, keep a journal or note pad just for this. Also, if you are doing this for the first time with tarot, start with the minor arcana and lower numbers and work your way up. The major arcana can be very thought and emotion provoking. They can tap directly into the psyche.

Samhain Meditation / Visualisation

This is the time of the year to go walking in the woods
If this is not possible then let the woodlands come to you
Sit comfortably and in as quiet a spot as possible and relax fully, as with any meditation.
If you can do this at night; all the better.
Visualise or 'see' with your mind's eye or simply imagine...
you are in a safe place – an open field is good
Fill all of your senses – smell the autumn damp air and leaves, feel the wind on your face, hear the wind in the grass and the trees beyond, maybe you will hear or see a bird fly overhead – what is it – an owl? A hawk?
Breathe deeply – inhale through your nose and out through your mouth, maybe you could taste the rain water from a leaf?
When you are fully in your space - start walking forwards - soon you will see a path - follow it.
This will bring you to a few trees either side of the path; continue fully immersed in the knowledge you are safe. As you continue on this path (does it twist and turn, or is it straight?) You will notice the trees getting thicker and denser, can you recognise any?
It is getting darker and darker by the step – but you are safe, if you need to see some light – allow a drop or two of late afternoon sunlight to filter through the treetops.
You continue slowly on this path and begin to feel a 'presence', a powerful presence but this will not hurt you.
Up ahead in the trees the path seems to end – but there is a small hill, only a couple of feet high, you feel the presence

strongly now and you are drawn to this hill at the end of the path, you are drawn toward this presence.

Before you you see a figure that comes into focus very slowly.

You see feet and legs and a human form clad in leather and furs; you notice a staff and as you look up there is a man with a heavy face and dark eyes; you are still not afraid.

Upon his head you see a patchwork of furs and above that antlers like that of a deer.

He stands mighty, powerful and tall, he tells you his name.

You are humbled by his presence and stand before him.

You ask him if you can be of help, or ask of him any question you need an answer to, remember what he says.

Once you have spoken give thanks and bow or cross your right arm over your chest – or do whatever is appropriate.

Walk backwards a while, until his image slowly fades away, only then, turn and walk back EXACTLY the way you came watching the trees grow smaller and become more sparse in numbers, until you are in your safe field again and finally become aware of your body and the here-and-now.

Yule / Winter Solstice Meditation / Visualisation

This is the time of the year to go out in the woods to collect yule logs, holly, ivy and mistletoe possibly with a large group, singing and causing general merriment.

If you cannot do this you can do a number of things, one of which is to 'visualise' going out in to the woods, alone or with others, and doing all the things we used to do.

If this is not possible then let the woodlands come to you.

Sit comfortably and in as quiet a spot as possible and relax fully as with any meditation.

Breathe deeply – inhale through your nose and out through your mouth. Visualise or 'see' with your mind's eye or simply imagine... you are in a safe place – an open field is good.

Fill all of your senses – smell the winter air, feel the crisp clean cold on your face, hear the winter breeze in the grass and the trees beyond; maybe you will hear or see a bird fly overhead – what is it – an owl? A hawk? Look for a holly tree and pay your respects, thank it for the life it represents at this time of 'death and re-birth'.

When you are fully in you space – start walking forwards – soon you will see a path, follow it. This will bring you to a few trees either side of the path; continue fully immersed in the knowledge you are safe. As you continue on this path (does it twist and turn or is straight?) You will notice the trees getting thicker and denser, can you recognise any? Is there any mistletoe in the branches?

It is getting darker and darker by the step but you are safe; if you need to see some light allow a drop or two of late afternoon sunlight to filter through the treetops.

You continue slowly on this path and begin to see a light in the distant darkness.

Up ahead in the trees the path seems to end but there is a small clearing at the end of the path - you are drawn to it, you are drawn towards this light that is growing in depth, size and brightness, but it is safe. Before you in the magnificent light you see something emerge from it – is it a figure? A symbol? Or something else? There is a gift waiting for you, is it a message?

Bathe in this glorious light, give thanks for all that is to come in this winter, give thanks for the gift that is yours. Honour that light and know it will be inside of you until the light of spring returns at Imbolc with Bridget.

Walk backwards a while until the light slowly fades away, only then, turn and walk back EXACTLY the way you came, watching the trees grow smaller and become more sparse in numbers, until you are in your safe field again and finally become aware of you body and the here and now.

Movement Meditation or moving meditation

'Trance dancing is a sacred rite, which at times embodies prophetic vision. It manifests the forces of nature, heals the sick and links the dead to their descendants. It assures us of our immortality, therefore providing us with direction and self-esteem. In ancient times it blessed the tribe or clan and returned it to a spiritual wholeness.

It is time for us to dance again.'

Frank Natale 1995

The one thing that helped me to meditate was Buddhism. I self taught and it aided me in the blanking of my mind and focusing on 'a spot on the wall' or on an image. Stilling my mind ensured the stilling of my body, however to dance enables the mind to quiet through movement. Even if you cannot walk, you are injured or even use a wheelchair you can still dance. I am familiar with someone who danced the 5 rhythms post-operatively. Of course if you are injured or had an operation (or pregnant) do seek medical advice before any exercise. Recently I seriously injured the ligaments in my foot, but I went to dance anyway, I danced on one leg, on a chair or simply rolled around on the floor. It was bliss and my poetry poured out of me in leaps and bounds, down on the floor or on that chair I saw the whole dance from a very different perspective.

So although society instills in us that meditation is about sounding the 'om' or being silent while sitting in a 'lotus' position this is fine if it works for you, if it resonates. If it does not that is not wrong, it is just not for you.

Dancing to a state of altered consciousness dates back over 40,000 years ago according to Frank Natale; many tribes and cultures still do so to this very day and finally it is reaching new heights of recognition in the western world, as well as all over the world. It is often referred to as ecstasy dance, however the traditional dance of moving to an altered state of consciousness is trance. Today you can empty that mind and fill your body, returning to the earth-body in order to reclaim your soul – or acknowledge it even further. Three ways I know to do this apart from actual 'trance' dance is Biodanzer, 5 Rhythm and contact improvisation.

'A life where there is love if often messy. Life without love is neater, but neatness is really preferable in bathrooms and written reports. Dancing alone is often easier and certainly less complicated than dancing with someone else, but there is nothing quite so satisfying as creating even one movement of real beauty moving gracefully with another. Perhaps to find this beauty more often, these movements of moving in exquisite alignment with each other and with the music that guides us, we need to let go of our ideas of what the dance should

look like and let the messiness of love guide us.'
Oriah Mountian Dreamer 2001

Walking In Nature

'We are all children of the Earth from whose storehouse we get our food... grown in the earth, fed with rain, strengthened by sunshine. Our cycles of sleep and waking are ruled by the cycles of night and day, our dreams are influenced by the light of the moon, and our health by the warmth of the sun.'
Marian Green

This bit can be put into three words 'get out there'. This can not be emphasised enough, go for a walk or a bike ride or if you have difficulty just get to a park or a tree and simply 'be' outside. Make sure you are prepared for the sun, heat, cold, wet weather - common sense of course; but always worth mentioning.

When you are out look to nature, simply look at one tree or one bush and look at it in every detail, every nuance - like seeing every letter in a word, every word on a page and drink in what you see. Tones, shades, bugs, soil, stones, damage, raindrops, try not to see the tree, but see all the aspects of it.

One of the most incredible meditations I have been introduced to was at Beltane, to look for a bee and watch it, getting down on the ground and 'look' at the bee, watch it get into a flower and gather pollen. It is like looking at another world, within a world. Just the other day a wasp landed on the patio table, I sat and watched it groom its antenna for almost two minutes, I felt privileged to witness a basic act and not have to recoil from a potential enemy. It looked so cute; the detail of this action made me see wasps in a whole new light. Do you?

Keeping things simple in a complex world

Living as a Pagan in a modern world is not the easiest thing for many. What with computers that fit in your hand bag, iPhone, iPod, iPlayer, nanotechnology and everyone wanting everything faster, it is difficult 'to get away from it all' or at least it can be. One small consolation is there are now train carriages with 'quiet' zones.

During World War Two the average distance between signals was eight hundred metres, now it is les than a foot (that is 12 inches or 30.48 centimetres). Thanks to the Victorians we do have parks. What I recommend is if you are going to be anytime in a city, research where there are parks, gardens or river walks and make a point in your day to get away from any tumult and freshen up.

Find a spot in your home where there is little to no mobile phone signal and maybe allot that space for craft activities or reading. Try and make a sacred space where there is no phone, fax or any electric items, or at least turn them all off at source – even pull the plugs out.

Try putting plants in your rooms, especially in your bedroom to cleanse the air, try aloe vera in the kitchen or bathroom (always on hand too for scalds and burns). Peace lilies are excellent for absorbing formaldehyde that exudes from new carpets and new furniture.

When you are angry or 'frazzled' just try and think of the earth, just remember what joy a patch of lush green grass, an oak tree or weeping willow by a river can provide. If you cannot go to these places in your day close your eyes and 'see' them, just stop for a *moment,* close your eyes and go there, if it is only ten seconds. If anyone asks what you are doing tell them you are simply strengthening your resolve; if your boss thinks you are flaking off work, tell them your only making yourself stronger for the rest of the working day.

If you use computers try having a talisman to keep them safe and healthy, helping to prevent negative vibes coming off them to you (and that way it stops negative energy coming off *you* to them!). Try a plant, like ivy which keeps in a small pot. Gemstones - anything black, tigers eye, snowflake obsidian or lapis lazuli; for yourself try white tourmaline if you are a man or black tourmaline if you are female (that is only a suggestion, you may try the other way around). Personally I find crystals are the best if you are using a phone a lot, and an ear-piece is a must if you are using a mobile phone for calls on a regular basis.

Carrying a talisman maybe 'old school', but you can not beat them, a tatty old coin, grandmother's brooch, a brass pixie or whatever it takes, every time your see or feel it in your pocket (or wherever it may be) it will remind you of one thing – its purpose. The power of thought is an amazing thing.

5. TAROT

Starting with the Minor Arcana is the best way to introduce yourself or others to the deck (the pack). A full deck comprises of 78 cards in total, this is then split into two groups; the Major Arcana, which has 22 and the Minor Arcana, which has 56 cards. The cards of the Major Arcana have pictures and numbers from I through XXI (21), with the Fool being '0'. The Minor Arcana is further split into 4 suits (much like that of a playing card deck). These are -:

Swords
Wands
Cups
Pentacles

All the suits of the Minor Arcana contain the following:-
Ace 2 3 4 5 6 7 8 9 10 Page Knight Queen King.

These 'suits' further have their own explanation, obviously

there are many books on Tarot and I am not here to write another one, just to provide a tiny outline introduction, and demonstrate how they are of use in ones Pagan path. Not all Pagans chose to use Tarot of course, it is up to yourself, there are of course Wicca decks, Druid decks, Pagan decks and so many more, a few are listed below.

Pentacles

These represent north, earth and work – including hard work; effort and even disappointment. Remember often a door needs to shut (even slam in the face) to see another one open. The 5 of Pentacles for example is difficulties and disappointments, in reverse it can mean enterprise or business opportunity.

Swords

The most archetypal of the masculine, although in Pagan ritual they represent the south, fire and unity. In Tarot they represent east and air. These further represent logical and linear thinking, decision making and plans. They then pertain to failure, doubt, success; even cowardice or triumph. Swords can also represent strength and balance (2 of Swords for example).

Wands

This is south and fire, these are sparks of wisdom, creativity intuition and discovery, often pertaining to a voyage, adventure and new horizons (for example 2 or even 3 of Wands). The Rider Waite deck's Wands have small little shoots coming from them, demonstrating a 'spark' of life, new beginning and even opportunity, creativity, a 'spark' of an idea, whether that has come to you at two in the morning or by way of a gift from the Goddess.

Cups

Represent west, water and emotions, frequently represented by the image of a chalice or chalices. The most archetypal of the feminine, these often pertain to the arts, deeper decision, position in life or relationships, friendship, love marriage, affairs (subject to interpretation by the individual) and imagination. The Cups often show harmony or balance (or lack of, but as with emotion it is not as simple as decisions that come from swords). Cups can go as far back as ones childhood

Further suggestions and recommendations

• Reverse cards do not mean opposite (do not worry about this for a while there is no need to reverse half the pack for a while)

• The images of Tarot – of any pack that appeals to you will show you their meaning instinctively

• My strongest advice is not to read any book or leaflet yet.

• Wait about 6 months, regularly perusing your Tarot first.

• Let your instinct come to you.

• Take them to bed, bond with them, shuffle them often, and do not share them.

• It is not essential but strong and legendary advice to wrap them in black or purple silk and place in the west of the room.

• However respect is the key and practicality goes a long way in the 21st century.

• Any deck is suited – whatever you 'feel' is right, whatever you 'feel' you could read.

- Beginners decks suggestions: Rider Waite Universal Pack or Pagan Tarot

- Not for beginners is the Thoth pack or convoluted packs like Baseball or Vampire.

Finally, please see 'further reading' for a tiny selection of books, however there are a great many out there. Tarot in Paganism is subject to interpretation, how one was brought up, what the images mean and how they make you feel in general. I personally had a slight fear of Tarot, even after practising Paganism for some time, I only knew that they were powerful tools and they were something to be revered and respected. I eventually found a teacher I could trust, from a workshop on a Pagan weekend camp, who guided me very slowly through a few details and cards. Through him and a couple of clairvoyant persons it was understood I had carried my fear through from a past life, now I teach the uses of Tarot to others. It is amazing how a fear can be turned around. However, my 'healthy' fear for the Tarot is prevalent and I cover them in silk, each deck has it own carry box or bag, I have a separate Tarot cloth for readings, but that is my personal way to care for them, you may develop your own, however all my pupils follow in my footsteps which is very sweet, often a pupil will emulate their teacher until they learn more and find their own way.

Tarot and Oracle Cards. Their Differences, Similarities and How to Utilise Them.

Although The Tarot is used for guidance and meditation as well as for day-to-day assistance, it is a form of divination taking the reader to many levels, even to an alchemical one. A reading can be done with as few cards as three (past, present and future) or even just the one to see what is ahead for the day, the oracle cards tend to be more unique to the individual and one card can say enough, more on that later. A full Tarot spread is often 9 (Celtic spread) or 13 for a calendar spread (12 for the months and 1 for the 'signifier' – the person receiving the reading), alternatively you could use 14 – one for signifier and 13 moons.

The signifier can be for a person or proxy, receiving the reading but not present, or a person asking for a reading on behalf of a third person, this is not the most ideal situation, but is not impossible, a mother for her son for example, personally if I can see it is out of genuine kindness and concern and not malice or vengeance or 'spying' it can work. Often signifiers are used for a reader to do a reading for someone via the internet or phone or mail for example. So it is a card that *represents* whoever is meant to receive the reading.

Oracle cards are just as deep, powerful and evocative, but their aims are more of a general guidance and the same card can have two very different meanings for two different people, there is a representation, a meaning to each, but they do not come from the same premise as a Tarot, each one has its own number its own suit and archetype.

If we look at the Oxford Concise Dictionary for a moment it

will show you:- 'Tarot', playing cards, five suits, traditionally 78 in a pack, used for fortune-telling.

If we look up 'Oracle' we have: - 'an infallible authority' or 'a response or message given by an oracle, especially and ambiguous one' or 'Priest or priestess acting as a medium for divine advice or prophecy in classical antiquity'

Oracle cards tend to be more soothing, more pleasing to the eye and are less likely to be shrouded in fear, depending on the deck they can be very beautiful and alluring, unlike Tarot that can produce trepidation and even anxiety.

For example if we look to the Druid Animal Oracle deck you will see a pack filled with creatures from bee to boar, from crane to dragon that depicts the creatures once prevalent to our native land, even those that are now steeped in fable like the dragon. They also contain the adder and salmon. All these can trigger archetypal imagery that is buried in our mind or psyche, for example the dragons will conjure up all kinds of legends, myth and stories. The 4 dragons are the strongest of the pack and are often taken out for learning and teaching purposes. All the cards have an alchemical level also, but are depicted in such a way one needs step-by-step knowledge in order to peel away all the oracle layers, Tarot on the other hand often taps directly into the psyche.

Native American Indian cards on the other hand depict animals, birds, reptiles and insects that are, or once were, native to North America, these show what the Native Indians of America refer to as animal medicine. As Druids see each tree as a medicine the Indians see each creature as a medicine. Each creature represents a story, and as with all stories contain a moral code to guide us in our everyday lives. Each one represents anything from dreams (duck) to darkest depths and shadow (panther), but ant and mouse are no less important.

Other oracles include I Ching cards, runes or rune cards, with almost every tradition having a form of cards or a deck, dating as far back as the Egyptian times. The Celtic Oracle dates back as far as 3 or 4 thousand years BCE (Before Common Era) where still today you can see ogham etched in standing stones in Wales and Ireland.

The ogham is a Celtic alphabet, but instead of letters like 'A B C' they had trees, birch, rowan, alder and others making 25 in total; however not every 'letter' is a tree - some are bushes or shrubs. The trees are letters carved as a line or lines on another line.

Other oracle cards include angels, dragons, goddesses, orbs, fairies, the Green Man, power animals (Celtic, shaman and Native American Indian) and many more.

There are no hard or fast rules as to how or what one should use as a Pagan, if you believe in angels – use angel cards, if you can see dragons in the clouds and you feel as if dragon energy 'speaks' to you try dragon oracle or Tarot cards. Ask Pagans friends what decks they have and if they can advise you or show you their cards so you can see how you feel, you do not need to touch them (as this may be a sensitive thing to many Tarot card holders) just ask if you may see them and ask the owner to lay a few down on their altar or Tarot cloth. Most Tarot holders (but not necessarily all) have a personal cloth – like an altar cloth – solely for the use of placing their Tarot cards upon, for divination, meditation and guidance - this cloth is used for no other purpose.

The goddess cards have proved invaluable to me in teaching –

even in a male-only environment and with male prisoners, they have been most useful as they give the viewer an image of the Goddess, these and many other decks like them are also great for anyone with learning difficulties or dyslexia.

6. STAGES OF LIFE

Birth (and a naming ceremony)

Where there is death there is life, and as the inevitability of loved ones and elders passing on to the next life, so new life is conceived and babies are born. Traditionally and (in my humble opinion, if I may) Pagans do not press their faith upon their children - biological, step, adopted or fostered, although they are a fundamental part of their parents practice and even ritual. All Pagan children descended from Pagan parents that I have met are not only given a choice to join in family (with or without guests) celebration, they are even encouraged to go to church, read or learn about other religions and even attend services of other faiths or religions. The choice remains theirs until they are old enough to make a formal decision (or any decision at all), usually after the age of sixteen or eighteen. I cannot say this is absolute, but it is certainly my view and I have thoroughly enjoyed a number of family celebrations.

When a Pagan or non-Pagan baby is born a simple ceremony can ensue, for example a naming ceremony or a simple ritual to request the Goddess look over baby and protect him or her until they are old enough to seek their own path. Sometimes a blessing can be performed on Mum and baby before the baby is born. In the native American Indian tribes a blessing is formed when the pregnant mother first feels a kick or a 'jolt', this to the Indians is an indication the soul has entered the baby in the womb, and so this is honoured and virtually unheard of in the western world. What is also lost is the tribal way women gave birth, it was changed to the ridiculous half-sitting position it is today (I am sure some Doctors will contest my saying ridiculous!). This is due to all doctors and midwives in about the medieval period being Christian, middle-aged white men, condoned by the church, so the baby can be 'blessed' in secret before it is entered into the world.

The tribal way (not to be confused with primitive) a woman would give birth would be to kneel down and lean forward, this matches the complex and angled position of a woman's anatomy. Native Indians would also build a 'lean-to' specifically for the birth, many if not all ancient (and one or two modern) traditions have birthing rituals, rites and blessings. It is also possible to be regressed to your own birth or even earlier when you were still in the womb, or; as I have experienced twice, a rebirth of your past life. Seek as much information as you can before doing this, meditate on it carefully first and if possible seek professional or shamanic advice, also try to appoint a friend on standby to talk to (or even cry profusely on their shoulder). It can be emotionally traumatic if you relive a difficult or traumatic birth, it is extremely healing however and can answer a lot of questions. Remember babies know everything when they are born, they are connected to the web of life or 'wyrd' and all knowledge, and they are still tapped into the collective consciousness.

There are no words in any language to begin to describe this feeling, however if you have or do manage to experience it you will feel a sense of completion and a deep understanding of humility and humanity (or at least its potential). One could go so far as to say, that it is no wonder that our ancestors believed in gods, believing in something greater than themselves, experiencing the above or being told these stories by shamans, without any other religion, faith, dogma or gender-bias being present.

A simple blessing would be to cast a circle and perform the details of a ceremony or ritual in the usual or chosen way, raise baby up to the north, then east then west then south (or the order in which your particular path dictates) asking for each of the elements to grant their gifts to baby, at the end in the centre or at the altar (take care with candles!) raise baby up to be granted blessings by the Goddess and God or Lord to protect baby and look upon him or her until they are old enough and wise enough to make their own decisions, close the circle or ceremony in the usual way. One practical piece of advice is to have someone neutral at hand, a guest of honour, not the parent or guardian or priestess or priest, they can be there to help and watch out for candles and sharp objects. I am sure any priestess will be sufficiently aware of babies' safety, but in ceremony consciousness and awareness does shift, a second pair of eyes and ears will never go amiss (and might help to assure the mother or father or guardian), just a suggestion. Personally I would, especially as it has been a very long time since

I have held a baby, I do remember they can wriggle!

Life and equality

A fundamental part of Paganism, if not its grass roots, is equality. All life has an equal right to exist, from ant, bee and bug to grandmother or tree. Male and female are equal also, in history many women worked and fought in battle equally alongside men. The best way I explain this to people is this: 'we may not be equal in this 'real' world, we may not be born equal, but we can *treat* each other equally or as equals', This helps to go a long way in explaining it to folk in this modern day and age, that is extremely patriarchal and class structured, or at least with an extreme division of wealth.

Every single step any Pagan has taken, to call themselves Pagan or desire to be called Pagan, even if it is misguided or through drugs or crime, or a Judeo-Christian background or upbringing, these steps brought them to the Goddess and if I am given the privilege of holding their hand (metaphorically and spiritually so to speak) then it is my honour and duty to do so. I hope that I have guided others likewise.

Life in Paganism is sacrosanct, there is no doubt many goddess or earth-based faiths of the past, even the Celts', made both human and animal sacrifices. We do not do this today, however we can sacrifice our time, our energy: dancing is a sacrifice, giving up an afternoon to be with a friend in need is a sacrifice, volunteer work can be deemed a sacrifice; it need not involve blood, but it can involve sweat or even tears. Even a sweat lodge can be a sacrifice, giving up doubts and fears, letting go of what you do not need any more, giving things away to others in need. This all pertains to the balance of one's life, to the community, to life in general. In Paganism we do not have the intent to kill or hurt anyone by words or deeds. No one human is infallible, but we can try, we can have the right intent, we can love and be loved, if we fall by the way side we can seek guidance and learn from our mistakes, and this will not produce judgment by fellow Pagans willing to help.

I will finish here with the first three lessons I learnt, that will stay with me for always.

We never lie, we never steal and anger serves no purpose. Now I add to that, all life is sacred and all persons are equal as human beings, as living creatures.

Death (and re-birth) requiems and funerals

In most aspects of Pagan faith if not all, death is life, where one door closes another opens. There is a whole practical side of Pagan death, including green funerals (eco friendly), practicalities, a general guide and legislation. Suffice to say you can legally bury a body anywhere except within about 125 metres of a water system, you certainly, no longer, need a 'funeral', a graveyard, a church or a minister, you can fully DIY a loved one's funeral.

Traditionally white is the colour for Pagan funerals, frequently or rather (so it is becoming) 'traditionally' called a requiem. A requiem is very basically a celebration of life not a mourning of death as if it is the end. We are immortal and our bodies, like stars and all things give out in the end! Our bodies to most if not all Pagans are but a house for the soul to which we can fully connect if we connect to the earth. In the end it will cease to function and return to the earth (or sky if you believe in the Norse or Egyptian mythology and have a funeral pyre so the soul returns to the stars).

If you have specific requirements upon your death like a requiem and especially if you are a solitary practitioner, you may, at some point, want to consider your wishes and appoint a guardian for this. I usually express my wishes to my long term partner, if that partner changes, I pass it on to the next one.

Some Pagans, but mainly to my experience shamans, can and do perform death rituals, to 'pretend' to die and be re-born. Some go through a rebirthing process. Sometimes even an initiation can be like dying, your commitment or sacrifice to the Goddess can be as practical and simple as giving up meat and becoming a vegetarian, giving up two cups of coffee a day and changing to de-caff and fair-trade and of course you then enact being reborn.

Death is inevitable but only our bodies are mortal not our spirit or soul. Pagans do differ in retrospect as to what happens after death. Most Pagans believe in reincarnation of one form or another, some witches believe in the Summerlands and reincarnations, other witches in only the Summerlands. If you have some experience with Tarot, try meditating on the death card, if not do some research into the subject - perhaps from a cultural or anthropological perspective. It is not morbid - it is actually healthy.

7. DRUIDRY AND WITCHCRAFT

Druidry

First of all please let me introduce the universal Druid's Prayer. This is a common practice for groves and hedge Druids who may meet up with other Druids in the community, or who have been invited to their grove. Some Pagan groups might recite it also, out of respect for their Druid members (welcome to a modern world!) You do not have to know it or memorise it, but here it is.

The Universal Druid's Prayer

Grant Oh Goddess Thy Protection
And in Protection, Strength
And in Strength, Understanding
And in Understanding, Knowledge

And in Knowledge, the Knowledge of Justice
And in the Knowledge of Justice, the Love of it
And in the Love of it, the Love of All Existences
And in the Love of All Existences, the Love of the God and Goddess
God, Goddess and All Goodness
So Mote It Be.

There is also a Welsh version, although this is subject to debate and translations differ, the most renowned version is one that is translated by Iolo Morganwg, however there are some slight variations, the internet will give you a number of options, or your local community or grove may have theirs.

Druids do tend to be different to Pagans – marginally, there is an onus on ancestors as much as, if not more than, deity. However, deity can play a major role of course. There appears to be more of a primal focus to the 'goddess' in general. They tend to start their ceremonies in the east, the direction of the bard and of the rising sun. Incidentally, Native American Indians face their tipi doors to the east.

Druidry is now an official religion, with charitable status, although Druidry is very much a way of life, a philosophy and spiritual practice.

There are three major areas of Druidry for contact and learning in the UK, the OBOD, or Order of Bards Ovates and Druids who have a full course of Bard, Ovate and then Druid, all by correspondence, run by Phillip Carr-Gomm. They provide residential and non-residential courses, a number of camps every year to include an Imbolc, Lammas and Samhainn camp. See further reading and resources for more details. OBOD describe Druidry as –

Druidry and Witchcraft

'Druidism, or Druidry as it is often called, is for some a spiritual path, for others a religion, and for others a cultural activity'.

For conferences on Druidry, run by Emma Restall-Orr and others there is the Druid Network, amidst a plethora of information on their website (you do not need to be a member to see it), there is a 'teaching' list, for those who visit schools etc. They also have a list of groups, groves and courses. They also have a tree-planting scheme and you can buy a 'gift' of a tree-planting donation, you can also get a 'certificate' if you would like your donation to be a gift.

Finally, there is a grove with courses run by Kristopher Hughes on Ynys Mon (Anglesey), amidst other things he runs a one-year course on Taliesin and speaks fluent Welsh. See networking for all further details and web sites under Druidry.

Witchcraft

'Witches are normal everyday people, the kind you pass on the street without giving them a second glance or thought. They are men and women of all age groups, who have all kinds of normal jobs and normal family lives.'

Kate West

Witchcraft is no longer an easy subject to define, like Paganism there are as many paths as there are individuals. We can put it in to two categories to start – hedge witch and coven member. A hedge witch is a witch who works alone, A coven member is simply a member of a coven, sworn to secrecy. In the old days a breach of secrecy could mean death for all members if they were found out and this was of the utmost importance. Secrecy today is still practiced but for different reasons and you will hear about people or friends saying 'I am a member of a coven' they may even tell you its name or where approximately they practice, but that should be it.

One definitive thing about witchcraft could be said – witches perform magic – or at the very least cast spells, and they do these spells or this magic in a circle they have cast.

'one of the most important basic beliefs…is the reality and possibility of magic. This involves the idea that the physical world is only part of reality.'
Doreen Valiente

Another common feature is to appoint the quarters (north, south, east, west). Wiccans tend to 'demand' the guardians or the spirits to the circle or ceremony, other witches tend to ask or invite. Druid witches *tend* to ask only if 'it be the divine will'.

Traditionally there are witches in all religions – certainly historically there are Catholic, Hindu, Muslim and Christian witches although little of this is written and almost nothing of it is now spoken due to the fact all monotheistic religions are patriarchal and therefore to grant power of magic (even by title alone) to a woman is unthinkable. Archetypically we think of witches as women, due to the old stories and images painted in medieval times, due to the masses of women murdered by burning alive, drowning or hanging not to mention starvation, disease or fever that was rife in the old prisons of the medieval times, where many people, men woman and children died before even making it to trial.

Historically I do not think we will know the full truth, but it is clear and written that Jesus performed magic and the Egyptians performed all kinds of magic, herbal lore, oil, animal worship, animal or cat magic, writing spells, pot magic - the list goes on.

Today witches, especially hedge witches tend to work with the environment. Pagan witches tend to work in harmony with the environment, they tend to be active in animal welfare, human rights and equality to name only a few. Of course not all witches are Pagans and certainly not all Pagans are witches. Pagan witches of course tend to follow the path of the Goddess – some Pagans and witches alike follow the sole path of the Goddess and leave out the Lord part altogether. Today witches work with herbs, learning and taking courses on the subject and even grow their own for food, medicine and make their own incense. Some witches go so far as to make their own paper (and further still some make their own ink or at least buy magic ink) and then do their own writing spells or enhance a spell by writing it down and burning it or burying it. Or of course putting it into their Book of Shadows – this is a fundamental part of witchcraft too – The Book Of Shadows. A book in which a witch – or coven, or even sister or brother pack may write their spells.

'A witch is a person who perceives vividly the connection between all aspects of life. Witches do not see spirit and matter as separate entities...They usually have a well-developed instinctual side. Also witches are vibrantly aware of unseen natural energies – which they use in their spellworkings...mostly to help and heal.'
Teresa Moorey

8. NETWORKING

Associations and finding others. Here is a list of companies and registered charities dedicated to helping all Pagans, Druids witches, Wiccans etc in the community. On the Pagan Federation web site click on 'districts' to find your nearest location for meets and events in your area, or see the green pages in Pagan Dawn (this is a separate insert in the Pagan Dawn magazine, not available, however, for prisoners until their release).

Pagan Federation the main charity for all Pagan communities, with the head office in London. Please feel free to write to them.

Pagan Federation Ministry sister offshoot governed by the Pagan Federation for all matters to do with chaplaincy (currently prisons and hospitals, although universities are now employing Pagan chaplains)

OBOD (Order of Bards Ovates and Druids of Britain) internationally recognised order for Druids with a correspondence course in 'Druidry' (through Bard training, then Ovate, then

75

Druid). Details on line at: www.druidry.org

Druid Network, run by Emma Restall Orr. Website: druidnetwork.org run by Emma Restall-Orr (Bobcat) emmarestallorr.org

The Llywyn Mon / The Grove of Moons is a grove run by Kristoffer Hughes,who is a fluent Welsh speaker and his first amazing book is out now, details, grove, courses and further links all available on his web site: angleseydruids.org

Children of Artemis registered charity for Wiccans and all manner of witches, those who think they are, or might be or even would like to be. Not all are Pagan, but many are, they have online and postal membership, they have an online shop and run courses, they run an 'International Witchfest' in London every year, they now also have a Lammas camp and many events. With membership you will get their magazine, in which are details of 'COA' meetings and how to run your own. Web site: witchcraft.org

Magazines and Outlets

Pagan Dawn the official magazine for the Pagan Federation. Filled with articles and all matters Pagan, the environment, deity and much more, with adverts on Pagan shops, current events, web sites, music and books.

Pentacle Magazine another long-standing Pagan magazine, with lots of great articles and details of what is current and going on in the community. Website: pentaclemagazine.co.uk.

Pagan Dreams a highly recognised online shop, now used nationally by the prison service (but not necessarily locally), fast and profession service at website: www.pagandreams.co.uk.

Wyrd Shop - based in Glasgow, Scotland. Their online shop is filled to the brim with all kinds of 'shiny' goodies, a great selection of Tarot decks, altar paraphernalia and cauldrons, hand-crafted athames and wands, there are umpteen pages for your delight, they also stock Pentacle Magazine and second hand books. Website: wyrdshop.com

Dancing:

5 Rhythms™ visit Gabriel Roth's site: Gabrielroth.com
For 5 Rhythms in Wales visit 5rhythmswales.co.uk. For all classes currently held by Alan Withers, correct to time of printing. He currently holds classes in Swansea, Tregaron, Camarthen, Cardiff and Machynlleth. Alex MacKay holds classes in Newport, Pembrokeshire and other parts of Wales. There are actually classes all over Britain including Scotland and Ireland, and all over the world, there is contact list on Gabriel's site including internationally registered teachers.

Biodanzer in the UK there is a website, from Elizabeth Barnett: biodanzabristol.co.uk

Antoinette Lorraine www.biodanza4all.com.

Contact Improvisation UK web site for Bristol:
contactdance.co.uk email: info@contactdance.co.uk and Devon - contactimprovisation.co.uk

Frank Natale has a trance dance institute. Website: franknatale.com

References

Dreamer, Mountain Oriah (2010) *The Dance*, Thorsons, London, UK
Green, Marian (2001) *Natural Witchcraft, the Timeless Arts and Crafts of the Country Witch*, Thorsons, London, UK.
Heart, George (2001) *Pocket Dictionary of Ancient Egyptian Gods and Goddesses*, British Museum Press, London, UK
Moorey, Teresa (1999) *A Beginner's Guide to Witchcraft*, Hodder & Stoughton, Abingdon, Oxon, UK
Natale, Frank (1995) *Trance Dance, the Dance of Life*. Elemental Books Limited, Shaftesbury, UK
Valiente, Doreen (1973) *ABC of Witchcraft Past and Present*. Robert Hale, London, UK
West, Kate (2001) *The Real Witches' Hand Book*, Thorsons, London, UK
Wilkinson, Richard H. (2003) *The Complete Gods and Goddesses of Ancient Egypt*, Thames and Hudson, London, UK.

I personally recommend all books by the following authors, all of whom I have had the magnificent pleasure of meeting and hear do a talk or presentation:

Beth, Rae (all great stuff for solitary witches)
Green, Marian (more great stuff for solitary witches)
Jennings, Pete (Pagan Paths and Pathworking are almost essential books to any Pagan collection)
Jones, Prudence (history)
Moorey, Teresa (witchcraft, astrology, moon work and much more)
Pennick, Nigel (runes, dragons, earth magic, history, Anglo-Saxon magic and history)
Phillips, Susan M. (with whom I have co-authored my first book *Green*

References

Living Sacred Life by Capall Bann) web site: capallbann.co.uk
Email: enquiries@capallbann.co.uk

Also recommended by myself, my peers and mentors...

Burrow, Stephen - *The Tomb Builders in Wales 4000-3000BC*
Car-Gomm, Phillip - *Druid Oracle Cards*
Cunningham, Scott especially if you are into herbs (he has two encyclopaedias), if you are a solitary practitioner or you want to make lots of magical stuff (oils brews and incense).
Farrar, Janet and **Farrar, Stewart** and **Bone, Gavin** – particularly *The Encyclopaedia of European Gods and Goddesses*, and *Witches Bible*
Green, Miranda J. - *Exploring The World Of The Druids*
Jones, Prudence and **Pennick, Nigel** - *A History of Pagan Europe*
Karri Allrich - *A Witch's Book of Dreams: Understanding the Power of Dreams and Symbols*
Sams, Jamie - *Native Indian Medicine Cards* (and guide book and journal)
Virtue, Doreen - *Goddess Cards*

Recommended further reading and more:

Formaldehyde (and cancer) website: cancer.gov/cancer/factsheet/risk/formaldehyde
The Mabinogion, various outlets original translation into English – Lady Charlotte Guest.
The Bread Book by Sarah Lewis published by Octopus.
Baphomet – Fact Sheet available from Raven catalogue
Raven – 17 Melton Fields, Brickyard lane, North Ferriby, East Yorkshire, HU14 3HE. Website: raven.karoo.net
Rider Waite Universal or Golden Tarot decks are great for beginners. Pagan, Witch, Wicca and Druid cards are available amidst many other Pagan styles.

Lightning Source UK Ltd.
Milton Keynes UK
UKOW04f0251131113

220956UK00001B/2/P